The
ARMS
RACE

WILL ANYONE WIN THE WEAPONS RACE?

Anita Croy

LUCENT
PRESS

Published in 2020 by
Lucent Press, an Imprint of Greenhaven Publishing, LLC
353 3rd Avenue
Suite 255
New York, NY 10010

Produced for Lucent by Calcium
Editors: Sarah Eason and Tim Cooke
Designers: Paul Myerscough and Lynne Lennon
Picture researcher: Rachel Blount

Picture credits: Cover: Shutterstock: Creativa Images (fg), Sergey Nivens (bg). Inside: Shutterstock: 1000 Words: p. 31; 1968: p. 14; 3Dsculptor: p. 11; Amagnawa1092: p. 23; Astrelok: p. 20; Pavel Chagochkin: p. 36; Cq Photo Juy: p. 42; Creative Lab: p. 21; DaLiu: p. 35; Dmitrydesign: p. 32; Manuela Durson: p. 12; Oscar Garriga Estrada: p. 28; Everett Historical: pp. 8, 18; GlebSStock: p. 30; Hadrian: p. 22; Dan Howell: p. 26; Hurricanehank: p. 27; ID1974: p. 13; Alexandros Michailidis: p. 10; Romanova Natali: p. 9; Nhungboon: p. 17; Sergey Nivens: p. 1; Photo.ua: p. 15; Lizette Potgieter: p. 25; PressLab: p. 29; R R: p. 37; Shujaa_777: p. 19; Sibsky2016: p. 41; Skyearth: p. 33; Keith Tarrier: p. 7; Mike Trukhachev: p. 16; Victority: pp. 4, 43; WindVector: p. 40; U. S. Army: U.S. Army Photo by Lawrence Torres III: p. 34; Wikimedia Commons: United States Air Force photo by Master Sergeant Steve Horton: p. 39; U.S. Air Force Photo/Lt. Col. Leslie Pratt: p. 38.

Cataloging-in-Publication Data

Names: Croy, Anita.
Title: The Arms Race: Will Anyone Win the Weapons Race? / Anita Croy.
Description: New York : Lucent Press, 2020. | Series: What's your viewpoint?
| Includes glossary and index.
Identifiers: ISBN 9781534565722 (pbk.) | ISBN 9781534565739 (library bound)
| ISBN 9781534565746 (ebook)
Subjects: LCSH: Nuclear weapons--Juvenile literature. | Arms race--Juvenile literature.
Classification: LCC U264.C79 2020 | DDC 355.02'17--dc23

Printed in the United States of America

CPSIA compliance information: Batch #BS19KL: For further information contact Greenhaven Publishing LLC, New York, New York at 1-844-317-7404.

Please visit our website, www.greenhavenpublishing.com. For a free color catalog of all our high-quality books, call toll free 1-844-317-7404 or fax 1-844-317-7405.

Contents

WHAT'S THE DEBATE?   4

CHAPTER ONE
THE ARMS RACE   6

CHAPTER TWO
THE NEW COLD WAR   12

CHAPTER THREE
NUCLEAR WEAPONS   18

CHAPTER FOUR
ARMS AND TERRORISM   24

CHAPTER FIVE
CYBERWARFARE   30

CHAPTER SIX
MACHINES AT WAR   36

THE ARMS RACE: WHAT'S NEXT?   42

THE FUTURE: WHAT'S YOUR VIEWPOINT?   44

Glossary   46

For More Information   47

Index   48

What's the Debate?

More than 70 years have passed since the end of World War II (1939–1945), yet many people remain concerned about the role arms play in the world. Warfare remains common, and weapons are increasingly powerful. Tensions between countries and the rise of international terrorist groups both threaten increased violence. Nations such as North Korea and Iran are seeking to build nuclear weapons. Russia is accused of trying to increase its political influence through a combination of military operations, and computer attacks called cyberwarfare. Many observers fear that such developments are making the world a more dangerous place. They debate whether nations should continue to try to outdo each other by building more powerful weapons in what is called the arms race.

This book looks at the debates surrounding the arms race. Read each chapter to find out about one debate. Then examine the ✔ and ✘ features at the end of the chapter, which explain both sides of the debate. Finally, review the "What's Your Viewpoint?" feature at the end of the chapter to make up your own mind about the debate. You can also find out what viewpoint people in leading positions hold by reading the "What's Their Viewpoint?" features. Let's start by taking a look at two arguments about the arms race: one in favor of weapons and one against.

Modern weapons range from small handguns to missiles that can travel thousands of miles.

DEBATING THE ARMS RACE

FOR WEAPONS

✓ Weapons help if a conflict breaks out. But according to some theories, the existence of so many weapons in the world actually helps prevent wars. They deter other countries from launching attacks.

✓ A country needs to keep up in the arms race to be able to defend itself.

✓ Any improvement in weapons by one country spurs a similar improvement by other countries.

✓ Smarter weapons will allow wars to be fought without huge numbers of human casualties.

AGAINST WEAPONS

✗ The constant creation of new, more powerful weapons in an arms race makes the world far more dangerous.

✗ The arms race gives too much international influence to superpowers such as the United States and China.

✗ There are already enough weapons in existence to destroy the world several times over.

✗ Future wars are far more likely to be fought by computers than by conventional weapons, so building more weapons is actually a waste of time.

CHAPTER ONE
THE ARMS RACE

For as long as countries have gone to war against each other, they have tried to possess better weapons than their enemies. In 1274 BCE, the Egyptian pharaoh Rameses II defeated the Hittites in the Battle of Kadesh because the Egyptians had more chariots than their opponents. In modern warfare, military commanders still try to gain a technological advantage over the enemy. Planning for combat is carried out as much in the laboratory or workshop as it is in military headquarters. Everyone wants to have as much of an advantage as they can if a war breaks out. Global spending on weapons and military in 2017 was a massive $1.7 trillion, as countries tried to assure their own defenses.

In March 2018, President Donald Trump signed a budget that included $700 billion for military spending, including 90 F-35 stealth jets, 24 F/A-18 Super Hornet fighter jets, and 80 AH-64 Apache Helicopters. Some people believe that such spending is essential. Without having enough defenses to destroy their enemies, governments fear that they will leave themselves open to attack. In this viewpoint, building up large numbers of powerful weapons is the best way of ensuring that they are never used. This theory is called deterrence.

A Different View

For other people, most military spending is a waste of money. Weapons technology is very expensive. Each AH-64 Apache costs at least $20 million. That is a lot of money to lose if a helicopter is shot down. Some critics of buying expensive weapons argue that the United States is now the world's only superpower. Its army is only the third-largest in the world, after China and India, but its

The F-35 is one of the world's most advanced fighter jets. Each jet costs up to $122 million.

weapons are so superior that it is the world's strongest military power. No one is realistically likely to attack it. Critics therefore argue the money is better spent on other things.

Other Debates

There are other debates about the arms race. One of the most important is whether all countries should be free to develop their own weapons technology. Currently, eight countries have the technology to build an atomic bomb. Atomic bombs are far more destructive than ordinary bombs. Supporters of atomic bombs argue that they are an effective deterrent. However, in 2018, President Trump met the leader of communist North Korea, Kim Jong Un, to try to persuade him to stop building nuclear weapons. Attempts by Iran to build nuclear technology also alarm many international observers.

Arms Races in History

Military theorists argues that the best way to keep the peace is to create a balance of power, in which countries have similar military strength. At different times, however, some countries try to gain an advantage. In the early 1900s, Great Britain began to build powerful battleships. To prevent the British from controlling the oceans, Germany also built more battleships. An arms race began that helped lead to the outbreak of World War I (1914–1918).

The buildup to World War II was another period of intense arms building. Again, Great Britain and Germany led the way. They each tried to develop faster fighter aircraft and more powerful bombers. The war was fought over huge distances and relied on hardware such as tanks, bombs, and submarines. The United States contributed advanced technology to the British and their allies even before it joined the war in December 1941. The industrial contribution of the world's greatest economic power was essential in bringing about the eventual Allied victory.

The British launched the battleship Dreadnought in 1906. This began an arms race with Germany.

The Nuclear World

After World War II, the world was dominated by two superpowers: the United States and the Soviet Union. The United States supported democracy and individual freedom. The Soviets wanted to impose a communist system on the world. The period of tension as both powers tried to increase their international influence was called the Cold War.

A nuclear arms race dominated the Cold War from the 1950s to the 1970s. Both sides built missiles to launch nuclear weapons at the other. They built enough weapons to destroy each other many times over. Military commanders and political leaders believed in a theory called mutually assured destruction, or MAD. According to MAD, both sides knew that, if they launched an attack, they would in turn suffer an attack by the enemy that would completely destroy them. Therefore, the theory went, neither side would start a war.

The United States invented the atomic bomb in 1945. The Soviet Union built its own atomic bomb in 1949.

WHAT'S THEIR VIEWPOINT?

Kenneth Waltz (1924–2013) was a leading US scholar of international relations. In 1981, he wrote an influential article entitled "Nuclear Myths and Political Realities." Waltz claimed that building more and more nuclear weapons did not make the world a more dangerous place. In fact, he argued that they make the world safer. If countries start a normal war with a nuclear power, Waltz said, they fear that the war will become a nuclear conflict. That fear prevents them from starting a war in the first place. As an example, Waltz highlighted the fact that India and Pakistan do not go to war, even though they both claim the disputed territory of Kashmir.

Thinking About the Arms Race

One issue that people debate when discussing the Cold War is that it did not end with the destruction of the Soviet Union in 1989. Some people believe that Russia, which was the most important country in the Soviet Union, remains the enemy of the United States and its allies in the West. They say that Russia wants to expand its influence in eastern Europe. To resist Russian aggression, Western powers must rely on military alliances such as the North Atlantic Treaty Organization, or NATO.

NATO was set up in 1949 as a defense against communist aggression. Its members committed to defending any other member that was attacked. Some experts believe that NATO is obsolete now that the Cold War is over. Other people believe that Russian aggression makes NATO more vital than ever.

NATO had 12 members when it was set up in 1949. Today, the organization has grown to include 29 members.

✓ KEEPING THE POWER BALANCE

Some people believe it is important for the United States to continue to have weapons superiority. In his first State of the Union address in January 2018, President Trump promised to continue to build arms. He said that to be fully defended, the United States must continue to improve its nuclear arsenal. Trump stated that he hoped the country would never need to use its nuclear weapons, but by making itself strong it would deter any acts of aggression from other nations.

✗ FORGETTING THE ARMS RACE

In April 2016, then-president Barack Obama wrote an opinion article for *The Washington Post*. It explained his intention to reduce the nuclear weapons in the world. This is called nonproliferation. Obama wrote that the United States had been the only nation to ever use nuclear weapons, and as such had an obligation to lead the way in eliminating them, but the country could not do this on its own—all world nations would need to be involved.

WHAT'S YOUR VIEWPOINT?

Do you agree with President Trump's viewpoint, or that of former president Obama? Use the prompts below to help form your viewpoint.

- Former president Obama admits that stopping nuclear proliferation will only be possible if all countries work together. How realistic is it to hope that this could happen?
- While other countries are building weapons, is it sensible for the United States to stop?
- If the United States does not stop building weapons, why should other nations?

Ballistic missiles can carry nuclear warheads to targets halfway around the world.

11

CHAPTER TWO
THE NEW COLD WAR

The Cold War set the United States and its allies on one side against the Soviet Union and its communist allies on the other. The two superpowers tried to spread their influence around the globe. They were openly hostile toward one another. Both sides built thousands of intercontinental ballistic missiles to threaten the other. Some of the missiles were armed with nuclear warheads. The United States and the Soviet Union did not fight each other directly, but each backed its allies in various wars around the world.

The Cold War ended when the Soviet Union collapsed in 1989. One reason for the collapse was the cost of trying to compete in the arms race. The Soviet economy could not rival that of the United States after then-president Ronald Reagan dramatically increased military spending. The Soviet Union broke up into its separate countries.

Cold War missiles were stored in deep pits, called silos, to protect them from enemy missile strikes.

The most important of these new countries was Russia, which had dominated the former superpower. The Soviet Union had been a one-party communist state. The new Russia introduced a democracy. It was a fragile nation, however. There was a high level of crime because some former Soviet officials seized control of former state-run businesses.

Putin Takes Control

Although the new Russia was a democracy, the constitution gave broad powers to the president. The first president, Boris Yeltsin, passed power to prime minister Vladimir Putin in 1999. Putin was a former officer in the Russian secret police, the KGB. He had led a successful military campaign against rebels in the province of Chechnya, who wanted to break away from Russia. Putin served two terms as president until 2008, when he became prime minister under President Dmitry Medvedev. Putin retained real control over the country. He was elected president again in 2012. He took steps to increase his personal control by arresting his political enemies, outlawing criticism, monitoring the activities of citizens, and banning regional elections. International observers said that Russia's elections were not free or fair. However, Putin remained popular with many Russians. They believed he was returning Russia to the international importance it had under the Soviet Union.

Some observers in the West were concerned at Putin's tightening grip on power. They pointed out that the old Communist Party continued to be popular in Russia. Putin even reintroduced the old Soviet national anthem. In the eyes of his critics, Putin had created a new version of the Soviet Union.

Even when Vladimir Putin stood aside from the Russian presidency, he retained real power.

Mixed Signals

Under Vladimir Putin and Dmitry Medvedev, Russia gave out mixed signals about its attitude toward the West. On the one hand, it began to work with NATO to help combat the growth of international terrorism. It also signed an agreement in 2005 to build a pipeline to sell natural gas to Germany. In 2002 and 2009, it signed new agreements with the United States to reduce nuclear weapons. In 2010, Medvedev visited the White House to ask then-president Barack Obama to support Russia's application to join the World Trade Organization (WTO). In many ways, it seemed Russia was playing a full role as a member of the international community.

Dmitry Medvedev led Russia into the WTO in December 2011, after 18 years of negotiations.

However, some observers also saw signs that Russia remained hostile toward the West. Putin angered Western governments in 2005, when he agreed to provide fuel for a nuclear reactor in Iran, which was violently opposed to the United States and its allies. In 2006, Russia fell out with Great Britain after a former Russian spy named Alexander Litvinenko was murdered in London using radioactive poison. The British blamed Russia, which denied the charge. Putin refused to allow the British to interview their main suspect in the murder. The following year, Putin pulled Russia out of an agreement to limit the number of heavy weapons that could be deployed in Europe. Tensions continued as the West continued to criticize Russia's treatment of Putin's political enemies, who were usually either jailed or exiled.

Invasion of Crimea

In 2014, Russian forces invaded Crimea, which is part of Russia's western neighbor, Ukraine. Crimea was home to many Russians who had settled there when it was part of the Soviet Union. Those Russians now voted to become part of Russia. In retaliation for the invasion, Russia was thrown out of the G-8, a group of the world's leading industrialized countries. In July 2014, pro-Russian rebels in Ukraine shot down a Malaysian passenger jet. All 298 people on board died. Critics in the West blamed Russia for supplying missiles to the rebels. The Russians denied this, but the European Union (EU) and the United States imposed sanctions on Russia to limit its trade.

WHAT'S THEIR VIEWPOINT?

Samantha Power became the US Ambassador to the United Nations (UN) in 2013, under then-president Barack Obama. She spent four years at the UN. In her last speech, in January 2017, she warned about the hostility Russia has toward the West. She said that President Putin's government was deliberately weakening the international order that had helped to keep peace in Western countries since the end of World War II. This order, based on shared rules and values, was at the heart of our way of life. She believed that the United States and its allies should work together to prevent Russia from causing instability.

Russian soldiers arriving in Crimea were welcomed by pro-Russian Ukrainians.

Interfering in Elections

In 2017, US intelligence agencies reported that Russia had interfered in the US presidential election of 2016. Groups who were either part of the Russian government or who worked for it had released false news stories and hacked politicians' emails. The extent of the Russian activities was unclear, but in February 2018, evidence proved 13 Russians and 3 Russian groups guilty. In 2018, the security services warned about possible Russian interference in that year's midterm elections. The director of National Intelligence, the director of the FBI, and the director of the National Security Agency (NSA) all agreed that the Russian threat was real.

President Donald Trump remained publicly doubtful about Russian interference in the election. He saw intelligence reports as attempts to undermine his election victory. In July 2018, he met President Vladimir Putin in Helsinki, where Putin denied interfering in the elections. Trump later reversed his statement and backed his intelligence experts. Many critics, however, were alarmed that the president did not seem to be taking seriously what they see as an extension of the Cold War.

President Trump backed Vladimir Putin's insistence that Russia did not interfere in US elections.

✓ STAY ON GUARD AGAINST RUSSIA

Dan Coats, the director of National Intelligence, told a Senate committee in mid-2018: "There should be no doubt that Russia perceives its past efforts as successful and views the 2018 US midterm elections as a potential target for Russian influence operations." He went on to say, "We need to inform the American public that this is real ... and that we are not going to allow some Russian to tell us how we're going to vote."

✗ RUSSIA IS NOT THE ENEMY

In July 2018, President Donald Trump met Vladimir Putin in Helsinki. Before the meeting, he told journalists that he did not see Putin as an "enemy" but as a "competitor." He added, "Hopefully, someday he'll be a friend. I just don't know." After the meeting, Trump said that he had asked if the Russians had interfered with the 2016 US presidential election. Putin had denied this and Trump seemed inclined to accept the Russian president's denial.

WHAT'S YOUR VIEWPOINT?

Dan Coats and President Trump take opposing views about Russia. Consider these points to see which view you most agree with.

US intelligence agencies are convinced that Russian hackers are seeking to influence US politics.

- Is President Trump right to consider Russia a "competitor" rather than an "enemy"? What do you think is the difference between the two?
- Do you think Dan Coats is right to say that Americans should be warned about Russian influence?
- What benefits might Vladimir Putin gain from interfering in elections?
- Why might Donald Trump trust Vladimir Putin's views more than those of US intelligence agencies?

CHAPTER THREE
NUCLEAR WEAPONS

Nuclear weapons are far more powerful than ordinary weapons that use gunpowder. Nuclear bombs create a chain reaction by either splitting tiny particles called atoms or by smashing them together. The chain reaction releases huge amounts of energy held within the atoms to create a massive explosion. The heat and the blast instantly destroy a large area and anyone inside it. The radiation released by the bomb travels even farther. It makes people sick and can kill them years after the original blast.

The atomic bomb was developed by Allied scientists in the United States during World War II. Two bombs were dropped at the end of the war to force Japan to surrender. The first, at Hiroshima, killed between 90,000 and 146,000 people. The second, at Nagasaki, killed up to 80,000 more. These are the only occasions nuclear weapons have ever been used in war. After World War II, US scientists developed an even more powerful nuclear bomb. This H-bomb uses hydrogen as the source of its energy.

After World War II, the United States tested atomic weapons on remote islands in the Pacific Ocean.

Nuclear Arms Race

After the war, an arms war began between the United States and the Soviet Union. The Soviets were eager to build their own atomic bomb. They announced that they had successfully achieved this in 1949. The two superpowers began building more and more bombs to target one another.

Meanwhile, other countries also set out to develop nuclear weapons. Their governments believed this was the best way to protect themselves from attack. However, developing nuclear weapons is very complicated and expensive. It requires precise scientific skill and uses expensive materials and machinery. Most countries simply could not afford to create nuclear weapons. By 1970, Great Britain, France, and China had acquired nuclear weapons. In addition, India and Pakistan have successfully tested nuclear weapons, and Israel is also believed to have done so.

The Soviet Union showed off its nuclear missiles in parades held to display its military power.

Preventing Proliferation

In 1970, most of the world's countries signed the Treaty on the Non-Proliferation of Nuclear Weapons (NPT). It limited nuclear weapons to the countries then known to possess them. These were the United States, the Soviet Union or Russia, Great Britain, France, and China. Three countries that did not sign the treaty have since developed or likely developed nuclear weapons. They are India, Pakistan, and Israel. In 2003, North Korea withdrew from the NPT after it tested its own nuclear device. North Korea conducted further tests after 2006. In September 2017, it tested a successful ballistic missile.

Controlling North Korea

The prospect of nuclear weapons being in the hands of a country such as North Korea alarms many observers, military planners, and politicians around the world. North Korea is one of the few communist states left in the world. Its people are highly controlled by the government, and are not allowed to travel abroad freely or access international media. Its leaders have often been critical of and hostile toward the United States and its allies. In turn, in 2002, former US president George W. Bush said that North Korea was a member of what he called an "Axis of Evil," which included countries that supported terrorism and countries that were trying to build weapons of mass destruction (WMD).

North Korea is run as a dictatorship by Kim Jong Un, who took over from his father Kim Jong Il in 2013. Kim Jong Un's coming to power made some observers hopeful that tension between the West and North Korea would be reduced. Instead, Kim increased the speed of the nuclear weapons development program. He was highly hostile toward the West.

About one-quarter of North Koreans are in the armed forces, known as the Korean People's Army.

A Change of Approach

Former president Barack Obama confirmed the US commitment to protecting North Korea's neighbors, South Korea and Japan. However, there was no further US diplomatic reaction to North Korean weapons tests. This approach was called strategic patience.

US policy changed when Donald Trump became president at the start of 2017. He encouraged South Korea and Japan to do more to defend themselves. However, when North Korea announced that it now possessed a ballistic missile capable of carrying a nuclear weapon, Trump warned that any attack would be met with "fire and fury." Some experts said that North Korea was still a long way from possessing a nuclear bomb that was a real threat to other countries. In response to further missile tests by North Korea, however, the United States and its allies imposed more economic sanctions as a punishment.

North Korea has conducted a series of missile launches around the world.

WHAT'S THEIR VIEWPOINT?

In 2015, the Iranian government was feared to be developing nuclear weapons. The international community agreed to a treaty that lifted sanctions on Iran in return for Iran promising only to develop nuclear technology to generate power. In May 2018, President Donald Trump withdrew from the treaty, despite objections from his allies. He said that he felt the treaty with Iran was totally flawed and that, by continuing to honor it, the United States and its allies would simply allow Iran to develop nuclear weapons. He felt that would be completely unacceptable, since he distrusted Iran and blamed them for helping terrorist groups.

Sanctions and Talks

North Korea was already poor after many years of sanctions. Supporters of further sanctions said they would force North Korea to stop developing nuclear weapons. However, other people argued that sanctions alone would not change anything. For one thing, North Korea regularly trades with its biggest economic partner, China. That limits the effect of any sanctions.

Some people began to argue that simply talking to North Korea would resolve the problem. In April 2018, North and South Korean leaders met to talk about formally ending the Korean War (1950–1953). By then, Kim had invited President Trump to North Korea's nuclear weapons program talks. After a series of hostile messages between the two sides, it seemed as though the talks would be canceled. In fact, the meeting took place in Singapore in June 2018. Both sides claimed that the talks were a great success.

The meeting between Trump and Kim was the first ever between presidents of the United States and North Korea.

The Americans said that Kim had committed to denuclearizing his country. The North Koreans dismantled a nuclear testing facility, and the Americans canceled the regular military exercises they hold with South Korean and Japanese forces. Some months later, however, there were signs that the two sides were again becoming more hostile. North Korea had failed to make rapid progress on disarmament.

✓ THE CASE FOR SANCTIONS

Diplomats have said the Security Council could consider sanctions such as banning North Korean exports and stopping its national airline and supplies of oil.

"Do we think more sanctions are going to work on North Korea? Not necessarily," Nikki Haley, the US ambassador to the UN, told a think tank in Washington, D.C. "But what does it do? It cuts off the revenue that allows them to build ballistic missiles."

✗ THE CASE AGAINST SANCTIONS

The Russian president Vladimir Putin supported talking to North Korea. He warned that the escalating crisis could cause a "planetary catastrophe" and huge loss of life. He described US proposals for further sanctions as "useless."

"Ramping up military hysteria in such conditions is senseless; it's a dead end. There is no other way to solve the North Korean nuclear issue, save that of peaceful dialogue."

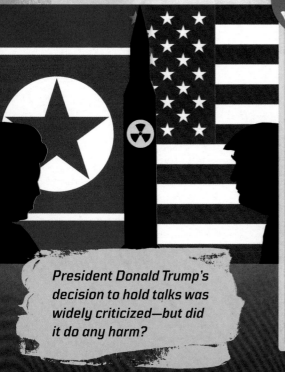

President Donald Trump's decision to hold talks was widely criticized—but did it do any harm?

WHAT'S YOUR VIEWPOINT?

Do you agree with Nikki Haley or Vladimir Putin? Use the prompts below to help form your viewpoint.

- Nikki Haley admits that more sanctions might not work. In that case, is there any point in putting them in place?
- What does Vladimir Putin mean by "military hysteria"? Who do you think he blames for the crisis?
- President Trump decided to meet Kim Jong Un. Even if the talks did not achieve much, did the president actually lose anything by trying to resolve the problem in this way?

CHAPTER FOUR
ARMS AND TERRORISM

One of the most pressing issues about the arms trade in the 2000s is how it is changing. Both the companies that sell arms and the customers who buy them are changing. In the past, arms manufacturers usually produced weapons for the country in which they were based or for its allies. For example, British weapons manufacturers often sold military hardware to countries in the British Commonwealth, such as Australia or Canada. This is largely the case today. However, the arms trade is a hugely profitable market. Many different companies compete for valuable contracts. This can lead to a situation in which it is cheaper for a government to buy weapons from a foreign company rather than one based in its own country. Some people believe this effectively places national defense in the hands of foreigners, which they claim is not a healthy situation.

In addition, the desire to gain sales leads arms companies to sell weapons to governments that many people believe do not share Western values. Weapons manufacturers in the United States and Europe sell military hardware to Saudi Arabia, for example. In 2015, Saudi Arabia led a coalition of African and Middle Eastern nations that intervened in a civil war in Yemen. Critics of arms deals argued that the weapons supplied to Saudi Arabia were being used against Yemeni civilians.

Countries may have a strategic reason to sell arms to a particular country. They may encourage arms companies to make trade deals. International relations can change, however. Countries may be allies in one conflict, and then enemies in another. In that case, they find themselves facing weapons they supplied.

Taking Action

Arms manufacturers themselves claim that they are simply
selling equipment. It is not their fault if the weapons are then
misused by the purchasers. In this view, arms companies are very
similar to any other manufacturers. They exist to make money
for their investors. The more arms they sell, the more money they
make. Supporters of arms companies argue that the morality of
warfare is not their business.

Hardware such as a new fighter jet or a new submarine is very
expensive to develop, so arms companies are usually eager to
be allowed to sell their goods to anyone who can pay for them.
Governments whose policies are generally rejected by the
international community are sometimes subject to sanctions that
prevent arms sales. However, it is difficult to get such sanctions
passed by the UN or other bodies. Even if sanctions are passed,
it is difficult to ensure that they will be universally applied.

*In countries such as
Afghanistan, many different
groups of fighters get ahold
of powerful weapons.*

Links to Terrorism

Some governments are associated with terrorist organizations. Pakistan was a member of the US-led Coalition in the war against al-Qaeda and the Taliban in Afghanistan. However, Western intelligence agencies believe there are close connections between branches of the Pakistani military and those very groups. That raises the possibility that arms supplied to Pakistan might eventually find their way to groups who could use them to attack U.S. or European soldiers.

In the past, the United States supported a group led by Osama bin Laden that was fighting the Soviet Union in Afghanistan. When bin Laden instead turned his al-Qaeda group against the United States, he had access to stores of Western weapons. Al-Qaeda carried out the 2001 9/11 terrorist attacks in New York City and Washington, D.C. About 15 years later, however, the United States was said to be sending funds to armed groups fighting the government in Syria. This included some groups allied to al-Qaeda.

Al-Qaeda was responsible for the attacks that destroyed the World Trade Center in New York City.

The black market is the major source of weapons for militia groups, terrorists, and criminals.

Black Market Weapons

Another threat is that terrorists can buy weapons on the black market. The situation is often particularly serious in places that have recently experienced warfare, such as Libya in North Africa, Iraq in the Middle East, and Afghanistan in Central Asia. Any conflict creates large stockpiles of hardware and ammunition. When a war ends, this equipment often ends up on the black market.

The collapse of the Soviet Union after 1989, for example, led to the disbanding of its armies. Many of its weapons became easily available in parts of Central Asia. The AK-47 assault rifle was originally manufactured by Kalashnikov for Soviet forces. After the end of the Cold War, it became commonly used by terrorists because there were so many AK-47s in circulation. They were also durable and easy to maintain.

WHAT'S THEIR VIEWPOINT?

Florence Parly became Minister of the Armed Forces in France in 2017. The following year, France was widely criticized for selling arms to Saudi Arabia. The Saudis had used the weapons to interfere in a civil war in Yemen with many civilian casualties. In response, some European nations limited arms sales to Saudi Arabia. Parly went on the radio to defend the French decision to sell more warships to Saudi Arabia, saying that at the time when the weapons were sold, France did not know how they would eventually be used. Parly insisted that France does not sell weapons "just anyhow."

Providing Arms for Terrorists

In November 2015, terrorists supporting the Islamic State in Iraq and Syria, or ISIS, group killed more than 130 people in an attack in Paris. They used bombs and automatic weapons. Their guns had come from military supplies left after the wars in the Balkans (1991–2001) in southeastern Europe. The guns had been smuggled across the continent. Other weapons have been used in terror attacks in Belgium, Denmark, and Sweden.

People responded to the terrorist attack in Barcelona in 2017 by attending memorials, such as this one.

Terrorism experts fear that terrorist groups have set up international networks to supply arms. The arms usually originate in legitimate deals between arms manufacturers and governments, but then pass into the hands of terrorists or criminals. Sometimes, however, they are supplied directly to potential terrorists. For example, the Central Intelligence Agency (CIA) sent funds and supplies, including weapons, to rebel groups fighting the government in Syria. Some of the groups were Islamic militants closely associated with al-Qaeda and ISIS. Some observers believed it was inevitable that US supplies would end up in the hands of these terrorist groups. That meant that money from US taxpayers was paying to support groups that have declared their hatred of the United States. For some experts, however, this was the best way to achieve the goal of defeating the Syrian government.

✅ STOP ARMING TERROR GROUPS

In 2017, the Stop Arming Terrorists Act was introduced to Congress. Representative Tulsi Gabbard said that the US government had been supporting armed groups linked to ISIS and al-Qaeda who were fighting against the Syrian government. She felt that, instead of spending money on such wars to overthrow foreign governments, the United States should rather work at defeating terrorist groups.

❌ KEEP SENDING U.S. SUPPLIES

In February 2017, *The Washington Post* talked to Saoud, who led rebels fighting the government in Yemen. The United States supported many rebel groups, but threatened to stop if they did not all work together. This seemed unlikely to happen. Saoud told the reporter that if the United States stopped supporting the rebels, the government of Yemen would be pleased, but the rebels would still fight each other until there was no one left alive to fight.

WHAT'S YOUR VIEWPOINT?

Do you think it is justified to cooperate with terrorists if it might help the United States? Use the prompts below to form your viewpoint.

- Tulsi Gabbard says the United States shouldn't take part in wars to overthrow governments in the Middle East. Why might the US government care who governs other countries?
- Is it morally justified for the United States to abandon allies such as Saoud who have supported its aims?
- Weapons from the Middle East are unlikely to end up in the hands of terrorists in the United States. Would your view be different if they were?

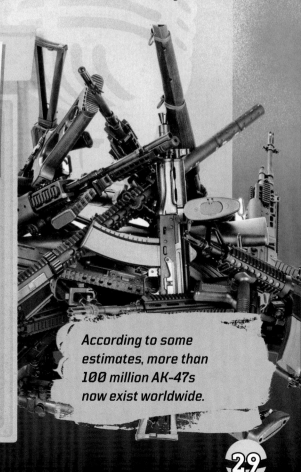

According to some estimates, more than 100 million AK-47s now exist worldwide.

CHAPTER FIVE
CYBERWARFARE

In the early years of the 21st century, some experts and military planners began to suggest that the whole idea of an arms race was out of date. The Cold War was over, so there was no longer a direct competition for military superiority. More terrorist groups and other "non-state actors" had access to weapons. Non-state actors are individuals or groups that are influential but that are not allied to particular countries.

Most of all, experts suggested that the idea of an arms race was outdated because it was based on an old-fashioned idea of warfare. In the future, they argued, wars would not be fought with tanks, aircraft, warships, or missiles, but with computers. This kind of conflict is called cyberwarfare.

Cyberwarfare is based on the fact that modern society cannot function without computer networks that control transportation, finance, and logistics. A cyberattack disables an enemy state and the activities of its citizens. It might hack energy suppliers to paralyze homes and workplaces, for example. This would lead eventually to an economic collapse. US law defines a cyberattack by another country as an act of war.

Cyberwarfare aims to disrupt computers that control systems that are essential to normal life.

Cyberwarfare in Action

The appeal of cyberwarfare is clear. Countries do not have to spend huge amounts of money on military equipment in a traditional arms race. They simply need to employ powerful computers. Cyberwarfare is also less destructive than conventional warfare. There are few, if any, casualties. There is also less damage to property. A physical invasion of another country might leave large areas devastated by shells and bombs. A successful cyberattack leaves physical infrastructure undamaged.

North Korea hacked the film company that made The Interview, *which mocked Kim Jong Un.*

There has never been a full-scale cyberwar. However, there have been a number of attacks that indicate how a war might be fought. In 2013, US officials suspected that Iran had hacked the controls of a dam in New York State. The following year, the U.S. Office of Personnel Management was hacked. The massive hack was traced to China.

In 2014, North Korea was believed to have hacked the computer network of Sony Pictures Entertainment. The company was about to release a movie poking fun at the North Korean leader, Kim Jong Un. The hackers leaked unreleased movies, together with thousands of private emails and staff social security numbers. The US government imposed sanctions on North Korea. However, a month later, a mysterious hack closed the North Korean Internet for half a day. Some observers guessed this might be a US response to the hack of Sony.

Russia at Work

It seems that Russia has already launched cyberattacks against its enemies. In August 2014, Russian troops invaded eastern Ukraine. The Ukrainian government protested the Russian occupation. The following winter, the power supply in eastern Ukraine was shut off for six hours. About 250,000 people were left without power in temperatures as low as 32°Fahrenheit (0°C). Russian hackers had used a type of malware called Black Energy to get inside computer systems controlling the power plant. Operators had to override the computers by switching to manual control to get the plant working again. The attack was just one of about 6,500 cyberattacks launched against 36 different Ukrainian targets from within Russia. These all occurred within just two months as the Russians tried to stop Ukrainian resistance to its invasion.

The Russian state is also suspected of using cyberwarfare to influence the U.S. presidential election in 2016. Russian military intelligence is said to have run disinformation campaigns using social media. It circulated fake news stories that were designed to increase support for one candidate or the other. The stories usually supported the Republicans, but in some cases they pretended to support Democrats to provoke Republican outrage.

The Ukrainian power system was a relatively easy target for hackers supporting Russia.

Hackers also carried out attacks on the Democratic Party's email servers. They stole and leaked hundreds of thousands of emails relating to Hillary Clinton's presidential campaign.

Hacking British Democracy

In 2017, it was the British who were attacked. That time, the source of the attack was suspected to have been either Iran or North Korea. Hackers used stolen security data to hack the systems of the Houses of Parliament in London. They accessed email accounts of members of Parliament and the House of Lords, as well as their staff. Security experts were able to shut down the hack after about 90 accounts had been breached. It seemed certain that the attack would have been far larger and more destructive if it had not been discovered when it was.

The Houses of Parliament in London came under cyberattack in summer 2017.

WHAT'S THEIR VIEWPOINT?

Ian Bremmer is a foreign policy expert and a leading US political scientist. In February 2017, he warned a security conference in Munich, Germany, that governments should be alarmed about possible cyberattacks from four countries. These countries were Russia, North Korea, China, and Iran. Bremmer said that the most dangerous of the four was Russia because it has the skills, and the willingness to use those skills, to undermine the United States and other Western countries. He warned that, in his opinion, Russia sometimes pays "criminals" to wage cyberwarfare, which makes defense against cyberattacks much more difficult.

Taking Defensive Steps

Defense against cyberattack is difficult. Hackers are continually working to get around online security systems. In 2001 and 2002, a British hacker named Gary McKinnon even managed to break into computer systems belonging to the US military itself, disrupting supplies. He claimed to be looking for evidence of UFO sightings he thought the government was hiding. The incident alarmed many US politicians and military planners by showing that even supposedly secure systems were open to attack.

US soldiers take part in a cyberwarfare exercise held in Germany in 2015. The exercise tested US cyberdefenses.

Meanwhile, the US Army has taken its own steps to secure cyberspace. Its new Cyber Command became fully operational in 2017. Cyber Command, which is based on the 780th Military Intelligence Brigade, is tasked with preventing cyberattacks on key US systems. One of its priorities is to keep open the computer systems on which businesses and individuals now rely.

Governments and organizations also increasingly practice dealing with cyberattacks. In 2017, for example, defense ministers from the EU took part in an exercise called EU Cybrid. It tested their decision-making during a simulated cyberattack to develop guidelines for a real-life attack.

✓ GUARD AGAINST THE CYBER THREAT

Sir Nick Carter is the British defense Chief of General Staff. In January 2018, he made a speech warning the British government of the importance of keeping up with Soviet military spending. He said that we have all now seen how cyberwarfare can disrupt or endanger lives, even in the United Kingdom. He warned that the people launching the cyberattacks were not thousands of miles away but "on Europe's doorstep."

✗ THE CYBER THREAT IS EXAGGERATED

Howard Schmidt worked as Chief of Security for Microsoft and eBay, and was a special adviser to former president Barack Obama. Schmidt believes the threat of cyberwarfare has been overstated. In 2010, he argued that too much time was being spent talking about "cyberwar." He felt that what some people called cyberwar was really only "economic espionage."

```
port socket, sys, os
int "][ Attacking " + sy
int "injecting " + sys.a
f attack():    I
id = os.fork()
= socket.socket(s
connect((sys.argv[1],
int ">> GET /" + sys.arg
send("GET /" + sys.argv[
send("                 argv
```

Some experts predict that cyberwarfare will be the biggest threat facing countries in the future.

WHAT'S YOUR VIEWPOINT?

Sir Nick Carter is a soldier, while Howard Schmidt is a computer expert. Who do you think has the most convincing viewpoint?

- There has never been a cyberwar. Do you think Schmidt is right to suggest the threat is exaggerated?
- When Nick Carter says people have seen examples of cyberwarfare that have disrupted and endangered lives, would it help if he gave examples?
- What do you think Schmidt means when he refers to "economic espionage"? Would that be less of a threat than cyberwarfare, or are they more or less the same?

CHAPTER SIX
MACHINES AT WAR

According to some estimates, about 123 million people died in wars during the 1900s. Such high casualty levels have inspired some military planners and engineers to envision a new type of warfare. According to this vision, wars will be fought by weapons that are operated remotely or that operate themselves. Soldiers are already being fitted with robotic exoskeletons, or frames, that allow them to run faster and carry heavier loads without becoming tired. Eventually, whole armies may be made up of robots that control themselves using artificial intelligence, or AI.

Although a conflict fought between machines would have fewer human casualties than traditional wars, the prospect causes much concern. Experts worry that such weapons would make wars more likely. If generals were not worried about losing the lives of soldiers, they might be quicker to launch an attack. Any robot attack might grow into a larger conflict that would inevitably involve human casualties.

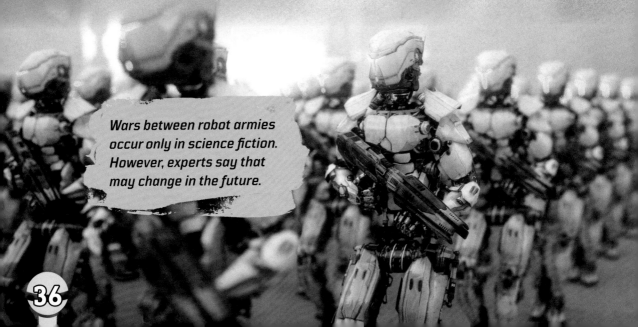

Wars between robot armies occur only in science fiction. However, experts say that may change in the future.

Bomb disposal robots carry cameras so they can be operated by experts using remote control.

Other experts fear the huge costs involved in developing such technology. Even a successful conflict could leave an economy in ruins. Other concerns are about whether machines could make reliable decisions about acceptable targets.

Uncrewed Weapons

Although uncrewed vehicles and fighting robots sound like something from a science fiction movie, they are very old. Ancient navies set fire to old ships and set them loose to drift into enemy vessels, which would then catch fire and sink. At the start of the twentieth century, the invention of radio technology made it possible to develop weapons controlled by an operator from a safe location. German engineers produced a remote-controlled mini-tank named Goliath during World War II. The Soviets had their own version, which was named the Teletank. The tanks carried weapons, which could be used to attack enemy positions without risk to the operator. The FL-boat was a remote-controlled German motorboat that was loaded with explosives. An operator on the shore steered the FL-boat into enemy ships.

During the 1970s, engineers developed robots to help defuse bombs. It was a period when terrorist groups in Europe and elsewhere began to use car bombs and other explosive devices. The robots were controlled by radio or by wires. They carried cameras so the operator could examine a device remotely and tools such as screwdrivers and cutters that would be used to disarm it. By the end of the 2000s, bomb disposal robots were far more advanced and could be operated from much farther away.

Unmanned Aerial Vehicles

During World War II, the German Army used pilotless flying bombs to attack targets such as London. The engines were programmed to cut out above a target, on which the aircraft would then fall. Since the 1960s, military engineers have been developing more advanced unmanned aerial vehicles (UAVs). Today, these weapons are better known as drones. They are either flown by remote control by pilots on the ground or are programmed to fly along a certain route.

Early drones were used mainly for reconnaissance. They were programmed to fly over enemy territory and take photographs of troop positions. In the 1990s, the first armed drone appeared. This was the Predator RQ-1L, which U.S. forces used successfully in conflicts in the former Yugoslavia, Iraq, and Operation Enduring Freedom, which began in Afghanistan in 2001. The Predator was armed with Hellfire missiles, which were effective against buildings, military hardware—and human targets. More drones followed, including the larger Reaper and the huge Global Hawk, which is designed to undertake missions that may last for many days.

A Predator drone carries up to four Hellfire missiles. The aircraft can stay airborne for up to 14 hours.

WHAT'S THEIR VIEWPOINT?

Bradley Strawser is a philosopher at the Naval Postgraduate School. In 2013, he wrote an article for *The Guardian* justifying the use of drones. He wrote that, if drones can accurately pinpoint their targets, they are preferable to other weapons, which risk injuring or killing a large number of innocent people who happen to be nearby. He argued that using drones also reduces the need to put our own soldiers in harm's way. In his opinion, if drones reduce loss of life, then they should be used instead of other weapons.

Drone Warfare

The advantages of drones are clear. Pilots are hundreds or thousands of miles from danger, in locations where they can be relieved when they get tired. The United States rapidly developed a large-scale drone program based at Creech Air Force Base in Nevada. While a fully qualified pilot steers the drone using computer controls, a team analyzes photographs and videos to identify possible targets on the ground. Drones fly so high that they are usually undetected until they launch a strike. The US military has used drones to carry out targeted strikes against suspected terrorists in places such as Afghanistan. A drone observes a potential target, while, at the same time, the target's identity is confirmed. The crew then identifies a potential time and location to make a strike. For their supporters, drones are a highly efficient way to target enemies of the United States.

Controversial Weapons

The drone warfare program is controversial. There are many reports of strikes hitting civilian targets, including men collecting scrap metal in Pakistan and wedding parties in both Afghanistan and Yemen. Critics claim that such cases of mistaken identity are inevitable. They say drone pilots risk becoming desensitized to violence, because what they are doing is similar to playing a video game. That might make them too quick to launch an attack.

For many people, drone warfare raises wider questions about the morality of warfare. For more than a century, warfare has generally been conducted according to a set of accepted rules called the rules of engagement. These rules were eventually written down in what is known the Geneva Convention. The convention outlawed the use of weapons such as gas and other chemicals. The use of uncrewed drones goes beyond the conventional practice of war. For some observers, this is a grave concern. It removes any idea that warfare is a fight between soldiers on the battlefield. A drone strike is an unexpected attack on an undefended individual by an invisible enemy. For critics, a targeted drone strike is morally little different from a murder.

Critics say the video images used by drone pilots make their missions like real-life computer games.

REC ▶ 3X TIME DATE ALTITUDE: 1297m FLIGHT SPEED: 1400km

TARGET 1
TARGET 2
TARGET 3
TARGET 4

✅ DRONES WORK WELL

In 2013, international law expert Benajmin Wittes, during a debate in Oxford, England, said that drones are an effective and desirable weapon. He identified several reasons why. Drones give operators greater certainty about who a target is. They allow operators to choose the moment to fire, minimizing unnecessary casualties. They reduce the risk of military casualties. Overall, Wittes argued, they are the best of any of the available options for targeting terrorists.

❌ DRONES DO NOT HELP U.S. STRATEGY

Audrey Kurth Cronin, a US professor of international security, argued in a 2013 article that drones are not effective. She admitted that they allow the killing of terrorist leaders. However, she said, that does not help overall US strategy, which is to get rid of all terrorist groups. Although drones might protect Americans in the short term, they are not defeating terrorist groups. In fact, they might be creating more enemies from among people who suffer from drone strikes.

WHAT'S YOUR VIEWPOINT?

Both Wittes and Cronin agree that drones are good at striking targets. Use the prompts below to help form your own viewpoint.

- Do you agree with Benjamin Wittes's view that one aim of warfare should be to minimize military casualties?
- Why does Cronin warn that drone strikes might convince people to join militant groups that are violently opposed to the United States?
- How do you think Americans would react to a drone strike against a suspected terrorist within the United States? Would such a suspect have a right to a fair trial?

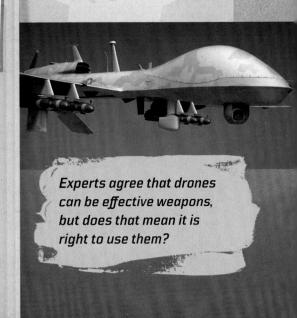

Experts agree that drones can be effective weapons, but does that mean it is right to use them?

The Arms Race: What's Next?

The future shape of the arms race is difficult to predict. Global politics are in a period of change. However, there are some key developments that will almost certainly play a role.

1 THE RUSSIAN PROBLEM

The international community remains suspicious of Russia's behavior. The Russian takeover of territory in Ukraine has left other European states on Russia's borders nervous. They want support from NATO, the European defense organization. However, President Donald Trump took office in January 2017, claiming that NATO was obsolete. He said that it was in US interests to have a close relationship with Russia. Other observers believe that Russia remains hostile toward the United States and its Western allies. They believe Russia will increasingly use cyberwarfare to disrupt Western elections.

The idea of nuclear weapons being in the hands of hostile governments alarms politicians around the world.

2 A SAFER WORLD

President Trump identified North Korea and Iran as rogue nations that were in danger of developing nuclear weapons. In summer 2018, Trump met Kim Jong Un to try to persuade him to stop his nuclear program. Trump claimed the meeting was a great success, but there was little follow-up from the North Koreans. Meanwhile, Trump withdrew from an agreement with Iran that it could develop nuclear technology only to generate electricity. He believed the deal would allow the Iranians to develop a bomb. U.S. allies continued to support the deal, but without US support it seemed unlikely to survive.

3 COMPUTER WARFARE

Cyberattacks are increasingly common. Experts believe that such attacks could be combined into an offensive large enough to be considered an "act of war." For example, modern military systems depend on computer networks, so disabling those computers would disable a nation's ability to defend itself. Disrupting financial markets could cause an economy to collapse. Armed forces are paying increasing attention to combating the cyber threat—at a vast financial cost.

4 BATTLEFIELD ROBOTS

The controversy over drone warfare may be only the start of a debate about the use of autonomous machines in warfare. Already, some warships are defended by entirely self-controlled cannons, which detect approaching aircraft or missiles and assess whether they are friendly or hostile. If it thinks they are hostile, it shoots them down. No humans are involved at any stage in the process. Military robots could possibly act in a similar way on the battlefield.

The Future: What's Your Viewpoint?

Some observers are pessimistic about the future of weapons and warfare. Others are more optimistic. These expert viewpoints all predict possible future developments linked to subjects in this book. After reading this book, who do you think is right?

WHAT'S THEIR VIEWPOINT?

Dr. Samuel Perlo-Freeman is a fellow at the World Peace Foundation. In 2018, he wrote a report on the conflict in Yemen. Perlo-Freeman observed that the Yemen war had led to an increase in debate about arms sales and in some instances had broken cross-party consensus in favor of arms sales in some parts of the world. The report stated that the Netherlands had been the first key European country to ban arms sales to Saudi Arabia. It also reported that the German government had made the decision to end arms sales to all countries that had been involved in the war.

WHAT'S THEIR VIEWPOINT?

In August 2018, two months after President Donald Trump met Kim Jong Un, experts at the UN reported that North Korea was continuing its nuclear and missile programs. It remained to be seen whether North Korea would uphold its apparent promise to discontinue its nuclear program. Mike Pompeo, the US secretary of state, remained optimistic. He predicted, "The work has begun. The process of denuclearization of the Korean peninsula is one that I think we have all known would take some time."

WHAT'S THEIR VIEWPOINT?

The Portuguese politician António Guterres became secretary-general of the UN at the start of 2017. In 2018, he predicted the growing danger of cyberwarfare. He said he was convinced that, just as battles in the past started with devastating cannon or airplane bombardments, the next war will start with a massive cyberattack to destroy communications and systems, taking away armies' ability to fight back.

WHAT'S THEIR VIEWPOINT?

In August 2018, President Donald Trump predicted that only sanctions would prevent Iran from developing nuclear technology. He said "We urge all nations to take such steps to make clear that the Iranian regime faces a choice: either change its threatening, destabilizing behavior and reintegrate with the global economy, or continue down a path of economic isolation."

WHAT'S THEIR VIEWPOINT?

Daniel Byman is a professor of foreign affairs. In 2013, he wrote an article for the *Foreign Affairs* magazine said that drone warfare would only become more widespread in the future as other countries developed the same technology as the United States. He also argued that the United States needs to have clearer rules about if and when it uses drones to kill citizens of other countries without them having the chance to stand trial.

WHAT'S YOUR VIEWPOINT?

The future of the arms race is complex. The viewpoints on these pages have supporters, but there are also many others. Even experts disagree about how best to control the arms trade, to keep rogue nations from developing nuclear weapons, or to avoid cyberwarfare. Use this book as a starting point to carry out research in books and online to develop your own viewpoint. Remember, there is no right or wrong answer—as long as you can justify your views.

Glossary

artificial intelligence (AI) the ability of computer systems to perform tasks that usually require an ability to think

atoms the smallest particles that can exist

ballistic missile a missile that flies in a high arc before falling onto its target

black market an illegal trade in things that are officially controlled or in short supply

chain reaction a chemical reaction in which a reaction sustains itself and spreads

coalition a temporary agreement of countries or political parties to take combined action

communist a person who supports a form of society in which the state owns all businesses

democracy a political system in which people elect representatives to govern them

desensitized no longer shocked by scenes of violence

deterrence the action of preventing an event by creating fear of its possible consequences

disarmament a reduction or removal of military forces or weapons

disinformation false information that is intended to mislead people

hacked gained unauthorized access to a computer system

hardware tools, machines, and other reusable equipment

intelligence agencies government departments that collect military or political information

intercontinental able to travel from one continent to another

malware software that is designed to damage, disrupt, or gain unauthorized access to computers

morality concerned with the principles of right and wrong behavior

nuclear weapons weapons that use the power held inside atoms to create an explosion

proliferation a rapid increase in the quantity of something

radioactive emitting harmful energy in the form of charged particles

retaliation the action of returning a military attack

sanctions penalties, such as restrictions on trade, imposed for breaking a rule

simulated imitating a real event

superpowers very powerful and influential countries

treaty a formal agreement between countries

warheads the explosive heads of missiles

weapons of mass destruction (WMD) nuclear or biological weapons that can cause widespread damage

For More Information

BOOKS

Anniss, Matt. *Cyber Wars* (I Witness War). New York, NY: Cavendish Square, 2018.

Burrows, Terry. *Robots, Drones, and Radar: Electronics Go to War* (STEM on the Battlefield). Minneapolis, MN: Lerner Publications, 2017.

Mason, Jenny. *The Nuclear Arms Race* (The Great Race: Fight to the Finish). New York, NY: Gareth Stevens Publishing, 2017.

Roberts, Russell. *Kim Jong Un* (World Leaders). Mendota Heights, MN: Focus Readers, 2018.

WEBSITES

Artificial Intelligence *www.wired.com/story/ai-could-revolutionize-war-as-much-as-nukes*
An account of how AI weapons could affect the battlefield.

Cyber War *www.npr.org/2018/01/27/579683042/5-ways-election-interference-could-and-probably-will-worsen-in-2018-and-beyond*
A page about Russian cyberattacks on US elections.

North Korea *www.bbc.co.uk/newsround/20692214*
A page about North Korea and why people are worried about it.

Nuclear Arms Race *science.howstuffworks.com/nuclear-arms-race.htm*
A history of the arms race during the Cold War.

Publisher's note to educators and parents: Our editors have carefully reviewed these websites to ensure that they are suitable for students. Many websites change frequently, however, and we cannot guarantee that a site's future contents will continue to meet our high standards of quality and educational value. Be advised that students should be closely supervised whenever they access the Internet.

Index

Afghanistan 25, 26, 27, 38, 39, 40
al-Qaeda 26, 28, 29
arms manufacturers 24–25
artificial intelligence (AI) 32–37
atomic bombs 7, 9, 18, 19

balance of power 8, 11
ballistic missiles 11, 12, 19, 21, 23
bin Laden, Osama 26
bomb disposal robots 37
bombs 7, 8, 9, 18–19, 21, 28, 31, 37, 38, 43
building arms 4, 5, 6, 7, 8, 9, 11, 19, 20, 23
Bush, George W. 20

casualties 5, 27, 31, 36, 38, 39, 41
China 5, 7, 19, 22, 31, 33
Cold War 9, 10, 12, 16, 27, 30
communist countries 7, 9, 10, 12, 13, 20
computer attacks 30–31, 32–33, 34–35, 42, 43, 45
Cyber Command 34
cyberwarfare 30–31, 32–33, 34–35, 42, 43, 45

deterrents 4, 6, 7, 11
drone warfare 38–39, 40–41, 45

Europe 10, 14, 27, 34, 35
European Union 15, 34

fighter jets 6, 7, 8, 25
France 19, 27

Germany 8, 37, 38, 44
Great Britain 8, 14, 19, 33

hackers 16, 17, 30–31, 32–33, 34
hardware 8, 24, 25, 27, 38

India 7, 9, 19
intelligence agencies 16, 17, 28
interfering with elections 16–17, 32, 42
Iran 4, 7, 14, 21, 31, 33, 43, 45
Islamic State in Iraq and Syria (ISIS) 28, 29

Japan 18, 21, 22

Kim Jong Un 7, 20, 22, 23, 31, 43, 44

Middle East 24, 27, 29
missiles 4, 9, 11, 12, 15, 19, 21, 23, 30, 38, 43, 44
morality of warfare 25, 40

North Atlantic Treaty Organization (NATO) 10, 14, 42
North Korea 4, 7, 19, 20–21, 22–23, 31, 33, 43, 44
nuclear technology 7, 9, 11, 12, 14, 18–19, 20–21, 22, 42, 43

Obama, Barack 11, 14, 15, 21, 35

Pakistan 9, 19, 26, 40
Putin, Vladimir 13, 14, 15, 16, 17, 23

Reagan, Ronald 12
remote-controlled weapons 36–37, 38–39, 40–41, 43
robot wars 36–37, 43

Russia 4, 10, 12, 13, 14, 15, 16–17, 32, 33, 42

sanctions 15, 21, 22, 23, 25, 31, 45
Saudi Arabia 24, 27, 44
Soviet Union 9, 10, 12, 13, 15, 19, 26, 27, 35, 37
Syria 26, 28, 29

Taliban 26
terrorists 26–27, 28–29, 30, 39, 41
The Interview 31
Treaty on the Non-Proliferation of Nuclear Weapons (NPT) 19
Trump, President Donald 6, 7, 11, 16, 17, 21, 22, 23, 42, 43, 44, 45

Ukraine 15, 32, 42
uncrewed weapons 37, 40
United Nations (UN) 15, 44, 45
United States 6–7, 8, 10, 11, 12, 14, 15, 18, 19, 20, 21, 26, 28, 29, 39
unmanned aerial vehicles (UAVs) 38–39

warships 8, 27, 30, 43
World Trade Center 26
World War I 8
World War II 4, 8, 9, 18, 37, 38

Yeltsin, Boris 13
Yemen 24, 27, 29, 40, 44